W9-BXS-603

CL

101 Facts About

101 Facts About

PREDATORS

101 FACTS ABOUT

TIGERS

Julia Barnes

Gareth Stevens Publishing
A WORLD ALMANAC EDUCATION GROUP COMPANY

Please visit our web site at: www.garethstevens.com
For a free color catalog describing Gareth Stevens Publishing's
list of high-quality books and multimedia programs,
call 1-800-542-2595 (USA) or 1-800-387-3178 (Canada).
Gareth Stevens Publishing's fax: (414) 332-3567.

Library of Congress Cataloging-in-Publication Data available upon request from publisher.
Fax (414) 336-0157 for the attention of the Publishing Records Department.

ISBN 0-8368-4041-0

This North American edition first published in 2004 by
Gareth Stevens Publishing
A World Almanac Education Group Company
330 West Olive Street, Suite 100
Milwaukee, WI 53212 USA

This U.S. edition copyright © 2004 by Gareth Stevens, Inc. Original edition © 2003 by First
Stone Publishing. First published in 2003 by First Stone Publishing, 4/5 The Marina,
Harbour Road, Lydney, Gloucestershire, GL15 5ET, United Kingdom. Additional end
matter © 2004 by Gareth Stevens, Inc.

First Stone Series Editor: Claire Horton-Bussey
First Stone Designer: Sarah Williams
Geographical consultant: Miles Ellison
Gareth Stevens Editor: Catherine Gardner

Printed in Hong Kong through Printworks Int. Ltd.

1 2 3 4 5 6 7 8 9 08 07 06 05 04

WHAT IS A PREDATOR?

Predators are nature's hunters – the creatures that must kill in order to survive. They come in all shapes and sizes, ranging from the mighty tiger to a slithering snake.

Although predators are different in many ways, they do have some features in common. All predators are necessary in the balance of nature. Predators keep the number of other animals in control, preventing disease and starvation. In addition, all predators adapted, or changed, to survive where they live. They developed special skills to find **prey** and kill it in the quickest, simplest way possible.

Stealth and strength combine to make the tiger the top predator in the parts of the world where it still lives. Although the tiger fears no other animal, humans are making it hard for the tiger to survive.

101 Facts About TIGERS

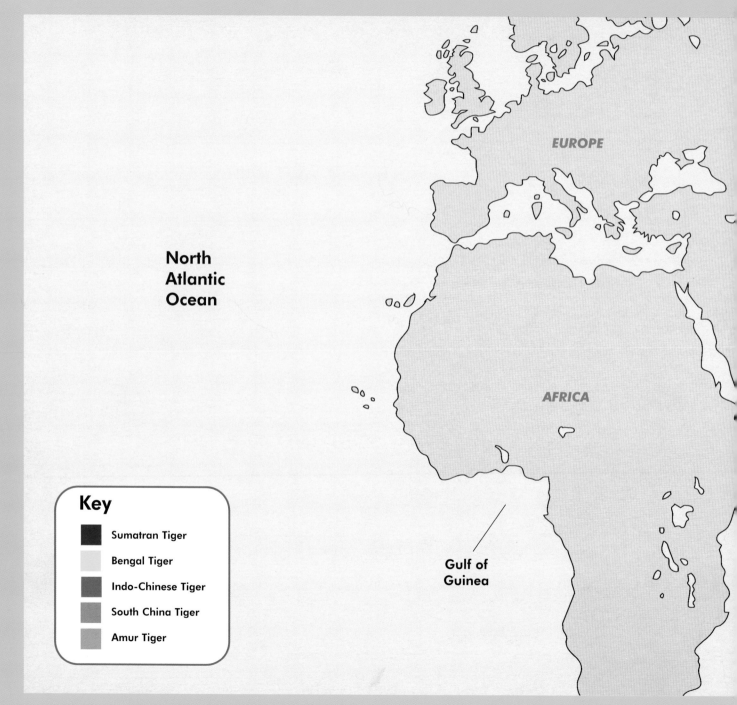

North
Atlantic
Ocean

EUROPE

AFRICA

Gulf of
Guinea

Key

- Sumatran Tiger
- Bengal Tiger
- Indo-Chinese Tiger
- South China Tiger
- Amur Tiger

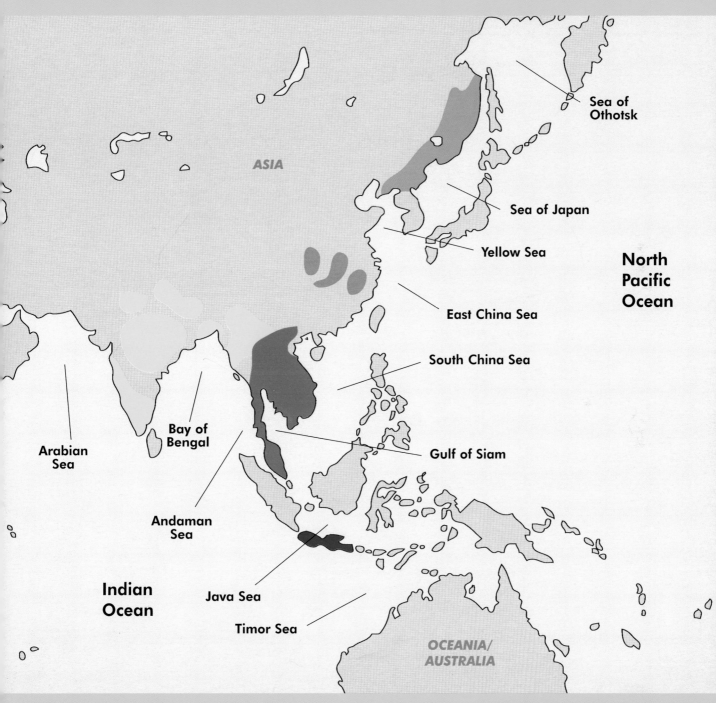

Sea of
Othotsk

Sea of Japan

Yellow Sea

ASIA

North
Pacific
Ocean

East China Sea

South China Sea

Arabian
Sea

Bay of
Bengal

Gulf of Siam

Andaman
Sea

Indian
Ocean

Java Sea

Timor Sea

OCEANIA/
AUSTRALIA

2 Over time, the miacids grew different from each other. Some of them developed features that are common to the wild cats that roam Earth today.

3 The group of wild cats has thirty-six different **species**. Tigers are the largest of the big cats, which are wild cats that are able to roar.

1 Tigers (above), hyenas, mongooses, raccoons, dogs, bears, and weasels all **evolved** from catlike animals called miacids. Small but vicious, miacids lived sixty million years ago and probably ate insects.

4 Five kinds of tigers still exist. They live only in some regions of Asia, such as Siberia, Mongolia, China, Indonesia, and India.

5 The Sumatran tiger lives in dense jungles on the small island of Sumatra in western Indonesia. Although it is the smallest of all tigers, an adult weighs 200 pounds (90 kilograms) or more.

6 The Siberian, or Amur, tiger (right), the biggest kind of tiger, weighs as much as 700 pounds (318 kg) by the time it is fully grown.

7 Tigers survive in many different places, such as the hot, steamy rain forest of central Asia; the dry, thorny forest of northwest India; the tall jungle grass at the foot of the Himalayas; and the spruce forests of Siberia.

8 The tiger has **adapted** to many different kinds of climates. No matter where it lives, however, it must have thick cover, such as trees or tall grass, to hide from prey.

9 The place where a tiger lives must have enough animals to hunt. The tiger's usual prey is deer, antelope, wild pigs, and monkeys. Large tigers may try to catch young elephants or buffalo.

10 The tiger also needs to live close to water for drinking and cooling off.

11 Tigers are the only big cats that often swim (left). A tiger can swim across a river that is 4 miles (6 kilometers) wide without any trouble.

12 A tiger is a **solitary** animal. An adult tiger lives and hunts alone, not in a group with others.

13 When a tiger hunts (right), it waits in cover close to a place prey visit, or it follows the trail or the smell of a prey animal.

14 A tiger cannot rely on chasing its prey. Although a tiger is powerful, it cannot run as fast as many animals, such as antelope or deer, over long distances.

15 To hunt, a tiger uses its ability to silently **stalk** its prey.

16 Patient stalking lets the tiger move as

close as possible to its prey. Then, at just the right time, it leaps into a surprise attack.

to fall. Then, holding the animal with razor-sharp claws, it sinks in its teeth and makes the kill.

19 Tigers must eat meat in order to survive. They depend on the hunting skills learned from their mothers and on the unique abilities of their bodies to be such successful predators in many **habitats**.

17 When the tiger has closed in on its prey, it sprints in a short, explosive burst of speed (above) and then pounces.

18 Using tremendous strength, the tiger strikes the prey animal's rear or upper body and forces it

20 The tiger's striped coat is one reason it is such a good hunter. The coat helps camouflage, or hide, the tiger as it stalks its prey. The prey animal may never see the tiger coming.

21 The patterns and colors help the tiger blend into different habitats, such as tall grass or a shady rain forest.

22 The base color of the coat may be any shade of yellow or orange, or it can be a reddish color.

23 Siberian tigers live in north China and Russia and must be able to hide in snow. Their coats are a lighter color (right).

24 Sumatran tigers are reddish brown and have lots of stripes. They can hide in the rain forest.

25 Tiger stripes can be any shade of gray, brown, or black. The tail is always marked with rings.

26 Like the fingerprint of a human, stripes identify a tiger. The pattern, size, and color of the stripes are different for each tiger.

27 Once in a while, an orange Bengal tiger has a white **cub** that has blue eyes. Its stripes are the color of chocolate (below).

28 A white cub often does not survive in the wild because predators can easily spot it.

29 A white adult tiger has trouble finding prey in the wild. Many white tigers are kept in zoos.

30 A tiger often hunts in the dim light of dawn or dusk or at night. To hunt effectively in low light, a tiger relies on a special layer in the back of its eyes that reflects light.

31 In low light, a tiger may see six times more clearly than a human can see.

32 The light-reflecting layer in the eyes of a tiger makes it harder for the tiger to see clearly in the bright light of day.

33 Whiskers help a tiger sense objects near to it. They also detect wind direction, information a tiger needs for hunting.

34 When a tiger spots prey, it stalks slowly

and carefully (above). If the prey hears a twig snap, it might run away before the tiger can pounce.

35 Soft pads on the bottom of a tiger's paws muffle the sound of its feet when it walks.

sound. Sounds tell the tiger where its prey is and how to plan an attack.

38 A sensitive sense of smell can help the tiger find prey, but smelling is not as vital for hunting as the tiger's other senses.

39 After a tiger strikes its prey, it uses its teeth to make the kill. The **canine teeth** have special nerves that direct its bite.

36 A tiger depends on its keen hearing to survive in the wild. Its ears are shaped like cups to pick up the smallest sounds.

37 As it hunts, the tiger strains to hear every

40 The tiger (left) has the largest upper canine teeth of all the big cats. They can be 3 inches (7.5 centimeters) long, about as long as the middle finger of an adult person.

41 Once a tiger kills its prey, it needs to find a place to eat where other animals do not disturb it.

42 Usually, the tiger does not eat in the place it kills its prey. It drags the **carcass** to a place that has thick cover before it eats (right).

43 Finding a good place to eat is so important that a tiger pulls even heavy carcasses to cover. A tiger can pull as much as thirteen people can.

44 A tiger was once seen dragging a full-grown buffalo 100 feet (30 m) up a steep hill.

45 When a tiger has killed an animal, it eats as much as it can. Then it saves the rest by covering it with plants or brush.

46 A tiger may be able to eat as much as 77 pounds (35 kg) of meat at one time.

47 In the zoo, a tiger must eat 15 pounds (7 kg) of meat a day to stay in good health.

48 In the wild, a tiger does not usually get regular daily meals.

49 Tigers hunt and eat alone (left). When one tiger makes a big kill, it may let other tigers eat, too.

50 Usually, however, a tiger must rely on its own hunting skills in order to eat. If it makes a mistake, it goes hungry.

51 Once prey animals know that a tiger is in the area, they run away or hide.

52 Some animals give warning calls when they spot a tiger. Their loud calls tell other animals in the area to watch out for the hunting predator.

53 When a tiger hunts, it goes away hungry many more times than it hits its target. About one out of twenty tries produces a meal for the hunting tiger (above).

54 A tiger usually has a **territory**, where it hunts, feeds, sleeps (above), and stays away from others.

55 A female tiger, or tigress, claims a small area compared to a male's territory. Her territory must provide enough food for herself and for her cubs.

56 A male protects a bigger territory. It includes the territories of several females.

57 Tigers communicate with each other in the form of scent messages.

58 A tiger has scent glands on its head and chin, between its toes, and at the base of its tail.

59 Every time a tiger rubs against a tree or branch, it leaves its own scent message. All the tigers in the area can detect and understand scent messages left by others.

60 A tiger also uses **urine** and **feces** to mark its area and to keep any others out (right).

61 By a scent message, a tiger can tell how old another tiger is and if it is a male or a female.

62 Scent messages tell a tiger to stay away from a certain area. In most cases, a tiger would rather avoid another tiger than fight it for its territory.

that its teeth are bared. This movement draws air over the Jacobson's organ.

65 Scent messages left by a tigress can tell a male tiger if she is ready for **breeding**.

66 A male tiger usually tries to **mate** with all of the tigresses that live in his territory.

67 Sometimes, more than one male tries to mate with a tigress at the same time. That is one of the few times tigers fight (left).

63 A tiger understands a scent message by using its Jacobson's organ, a special scent center in the roof of its mouth that detects chemical traces in the air.

64 To take in as much scent as possible, a tiger lifts its head, wrinkles its nose, and curls up its lips so

68 Angry tigers growl and snarl and may hiss at their enemies.

69 Roaring warns other tigers to keep away or helps to attract a mate. A roar can be heard for up to 2 miles (3 km).

70 The male tiger stays with the tigress for a few days during the mating period (below). Then the two tigers separate again.

71 Male tigers play no part in the birth or care of the couple's cubs.

72 While the tigress is **pregnant**, she must hunt for herself. She gets no help from other tigers.

73 The tigress does not have to wait long for her cubs to arrive. They are born about fifteen weeks after she mates (above).

74 When it is time for her to give birth, the tigress finds a **den**. A good den must have enough cover to hide her young, be close to water, and give her a view so she can spot danger.

75 A tiger's **litter** is small. Usually, two

or three cubs are born at one time. A tiger can have up to five cubs in a litter.

76 Cubs cannot open their eyes right after they are born. In about one week, their eyes open, and they see for the first time.

77 The tiger cubs drink only their mother's milk for the first two months of their lives.

78 A tigress still must hunt for herself. While she is

gone, the cubs are alone in the den (below).

79 When the tigress is gone from the den, the cubs are in danger. The cubs would make easy prey for another predator, such as a wild dog.

80 If the mother senses danger, she moves to a new den. She picks up each cub in turn and carries it to a new home.

81 By the time they are four weeks old, the cubs (below) get their first set of teeth. These small, sharp teeth are called milk teeth.

82 The cubs usually taste meat for the first time after they are two months old.

83 For their first meals, the mother makes kills near the den and takes the cubs to the carcasses.

84 While they are small, cubs rely on their

mother for all their food. She works hard to catch enough prey for herself and her young cubs.

85 As the cubs grow, they leave the safety of the den to join their mother on her hunting trips.

86 The cubs are more of a nuisance than a help on their first hunting trips. They are noisy, clumsy, and playful (right). They may even scare away prey.

87 Taking the cubs on a hunting trip does have one advantage. When the cubs are with the mother, she does not have to return to the den so often. She can travel farther and use all her territory to search for food.

during their first few months of life. After they turn one year old (left), they may spend longer periods of time on their own away from the den.

90 The cubs are ready to live alone when they are about two years old.

88 As the cubs watch their mother, they learn how to hunt. Step by step, they try to catch and kill their prey.

89 The cubs hunt, play, and sleep together

91 A female cub often sets up her territory quite close to the territory of her mother. Finding territory is harder for a male.

92 At first, a male may have trouble finding land that does not belong to another male. Males wander between territories and try to avoid older male tigers.

93 Each male tries to carve out a territory of his own. Each one needs a hunting area of his own in order to find enough prey to feed himself.

94 Land for hunting is hard to find. People have turned land once used by tigers into farm fields and built homes there.

95 People want to keep tigers as far away from their farms as possible. Tigers have preyed on farm animals (below).

96 Humans hunt and kill tigers for their skins, even though selling them is illegal. Body parts, such as whiskers (below), are used in traditional medicine.

97 Some countries ban tiger hunting or set up special areas where tigers can live. Still, tigers struggle to survive in the wild.

98 Three types of tigers could not survive. The Bali, the Caspian, and the Javan tigers are already **extinct**. The Siberian, South China, Indo-Chinese, Bengal, and Sumatran tigers remain in small numbers.

99 From five thousand to seven thousand tigers remain in the world's shrinking wild areas.

100 The most common tiger is the Bengal, or Indian, tiger. The most **endangered** tiger is the South China tiger; fewer than thirty are left in the wild.

101 If humans cannot do a better job of sharing land with tigers, all of the tigers may die out in the wild. The tiger (right), a majestic and independent predator, would survive only in the cages of zoos.

Glossary

adapted: changed or adjusted.

breeding: producing and bearing young.

canine teeth: sharp, pointed teeth used for biting and killing.

carcass: the body of a dead animal.

cub: a young mammal, such as a bear, fox, or tiger.

den: a place where a tigress gives birth and cares for her cubs.

endangered: in danger of dying out in the wild.

evolved: changed or developed, usually over a long period of time.

extinct: having none of its kind left.

feces: an animal's droppings.

habitats: places where a plant or animal is usually found.

litter: a group of young born to the same mother at the same time.

mate: to have a male and female come together to produce young.

predators: animals that kill other animals for food.

pregnant: having young growing inside a female's body.

prey: the animal a predator picks to hunt and kill.

solitary: being or living alone.

species: types of animals or plants that are alike in many ways.

stalk: to sneak up on prey.

territory: an area where an animal lives and hunts.

urine: an animal's liquid waste.

More Books to Read

Tiger (*Animal Saver* series)
Samantha Beres
(Dutton)

Tigers (*Big Cats* series)
Victor Gentle and Janet Perry
(Gareth Stevens)

Tiger (*Natural World* series)
Bill Jordan and Valmik Thapar
(Raintree/Steck-Vaughn)

Tigers (*Early Bird Nature Books* series)
Lesley A. DuTemple
(Lerner)

Web Sites

Big Cats
www.bigcats.com

Tiger Information Center Kids' Page
www.5tigers.org/Directory/kids.htm

Eyes on the Tiger
www.nationalgeographic.com/geoguide/tigers

Tiger Territory
www.lairweb.org.nz/tiger/

To find additional web sites, use a reliable search engine to find one or more of the following keywords: **Bengal tiger, big cats, tigers**.

Index